Kē jī quǎn de nuǎn xīn zhēn yán

柯基犬的暖心箴言

Corgi
State of
Mind

by Katrina Liu   Illustrated by Eve Farb

Scan to listen to
the audio reading!

For free printables and more books by Katrina liu visit

MINALEARNSCHINESE.COM

@minalearnschinese

ABOUT THE AUTHOR

Katrina Liu is an American-born Taiwanese/Chinese mom and children's book author from San Francisco, California. She lives with her husband, 2 daughters, and dog, Musubi, and is passionate about amplifying Asian-American stories and sharing Asian culture with the world. She's written several books including bilingual children's books in Chinese and English, intended to support non-native speaking families.

For Mina & Leah

ISBN: 978-1-953281-65-4

嘿，開心做自己吧！

沒有人比你更適合做"你"。

跟我來吧！你一定會覺得好玩。

讓我們一起大聲說。

Hey there! Be yourself.
There's really no one better.
Come with me. It's fun! You'll see.
Let's say these things together.

Jīn tiān huì shì méi hǎo de yì tiān! Wó yǒu mǎn mǎn de ài hé guī shú gǎn.

今天會是美好的一天！我有滿滿的愛和歸屬感。

Today will be a great day! I am loved, and I belong.

我吃健康、有營養的食物，讓身體強壯。

Wǒ chī jiàn kāng, yǒu yíng yǎng de shí wù, ràng shēn tǐ qiáng zhuàng.

I eat healthy, nutritious foods to keep my body strong.

Wǒ chōng mǎn zì xìn, áng shǒu kuò bù.

我充滿自信，昂首闊步。

I am confident and walk
tall with every stride.

Wó bǎo hù wǒ de yuán zé.

我保護我的原則。

Méi cuò, wǒ de yuán zé wǒ shuō le suàn.

沒錯，我的原則我說了算。

I protect my boundaries.
— Yes, they're mine to decide.

Wǒ duì rén yǒu shàn, xǐ huān qù liǎo jiě tā men.
我對人友善，喜歡去了解他們。
I am kind to others and love learning what they're about.

Wó zhǐ xī rù jī jí de xiáng fǎ,
我只吸入積極的想法，
hū chū suó yǒu de bù ān.
呼出所有的不安。
I breathe in only good thoughts
and exhale out all my doubts.

Wǒ bú hài pà,   huì yóng gǎn de ràng zì   jí shǎn liàng.

我不害怕，會勇敢地讓自己閃亮。

I'm not afraid to make a splash no matter how big or small.

Wǒ néng kè fú rèn hé fēng yǔ,

我能克服任何風雨，

měi cì diē dǎo le dōu huì chóng xīn zhàn qǐ lái.

每次跌倒了都會重新站起來。

I can weather any storm and get back up each time I fall.

Jīng cǎi de shì jiè děng zhe wǒ qù tàn suǒ.

精彩的世界等著我去探索。

Wǒ huì jìn qíng cháng shì xīn shì wù.

我會盡情嘗試新事物。

Exciting adventures are ahead. There's nothing I won't try.

Wǒ de rén shēng wǒ zuò zhǔ.
我的人生我做主。
Zhè shì wǒ jiān dìng bù yí de xìn niàn.
這是我堅定不移的信念。
I'm the captain of my ship.
That's the motto I live by.

Wǒ yuàn yì jié jiāo gēn wǒ bù yí yàng de xīn péng yǒu.

我願意結交跟我不一樣的新朋友。

I'm open to making new friends who are different from me.

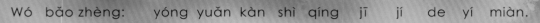

Wó bǎo zhèng: yóng yuǎn kàn shì qíng jī jí de yí miàn.

我保證：永遠看事情積極的一面。

I'll always see the brighter side, and that's a guarantee!

Wó gǎn ēn jīn tiān de yí qiè.　　Wǒ yòng xīn zuò hǎo měi yí jiàn shì.

我感恩今天的一切。我用心做好每一件事。

Xiàn zài gāi shàng chuáng shuì jiào le.　　Wǒ zhí dé hǎo hǎo shuì yí jiào.

現在該上床睡覺了。我值得好好睡一覺。

I am grateful for today. I did my very best!
Now it's time to head to bed. I deserve a good night's rest.

Collect them all!

MINALEARNSCHINESE.COM

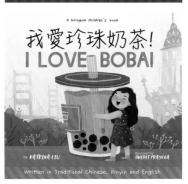

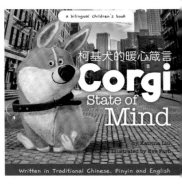